Copyright © 1987 Editions du Centurion.
English text translation © 1991 Picture Book Studio.
Published by Picture Book Studio, Saxonville, MA.
Distributed in Canada by Vanwell Publishing, St. Catharines, Ont.
All rights reserved.
Printed in Hong Kong.
10 9 8 7 6 5 4 3 2 1

Library of Congress Cataloging in Publication Data
Beaude, Pierre-Marie.
[Livre de la Création. English]
The Book of Creation / by Pierre-Marie Beaude; illustrated by Georges Lemoine.
Translation of : Le livre de la Création.
Summary: Presents an illustrated version of the Creation story as it may have been told by a father to his son in the land of Canaan 2500 years ago.
ISBN 0-88708-141-X : $16.95
1. Creation—Juvenile literature. [1. Creation. 2. Bible stories—O.T.] I. Lemoine, Georges, ill. II. Title.
BS652.B3613   1990
222'.1109505—dc20   90-35418

THE BOOK OF CREATION

Written by Pierre-Marie Beaude   Illustrated by Georges Lemoine

Translated by Andrew Clements

Picture Book Studio

IN THE BEGINNING…

In the land of Canaan
two thousand five hundred years ago,
there are two shepherds—a father and son.
The father's name is Eliezer and his son is Jonathan.

The evening sun had set, but it was still bright enough to see the desert clearly. Eliezer and Jonathan shared their supper of bread, curds, and figs. In front of them was a stone pen for their sheep and goats. There were several newborn lambs and kids, and they would have to be carefully looked after during the night…

Jonathan loved these long evenings spent alone with his father, several hours' walk from the main camp. They ate in silence, just watching the night. Then Eliezer put the bread into a bag and hung it from a shepherd staff stuck into the sand to keep it away from the little desert insects.

Next he chose a large flat stone to sit on, and pulled his cloak up over his knees. Jonathan found himself a sitting stone there next to his father. He knew that soon they would talk, just the two of them together. Eliezer would tell him things he had learned long ago from his own father. He would teach him again about being a good shepherd, and about avoiding the dangers of the beautiful desert.

There was one story that Jonathan wanted to hear: the story of how the world began. Several times before he had asked his father to tell it to him, but Eliezer had always said, "This story is different from all the others; it will take you a long time to get ready to hear it."

"Why?" Jonathan had always asked.

And Eliezer had always replied, "There are secrets in this story—hidden like water in the earth—all the secrets of how we came to be living beings."

So, Jonathan had begun to prepare himself to hear this story. This preparation was not complicated or difficult. Jonathan just paid more attention than usual to everything he saw around him—like a bird flying across the sky, or a gently swaying blade of grass. He also listened to everything with much greater care, and he caught sounds he had never heard before: the wind among the stones, for instance, or even the faint whistling that the air makes when a person breathes.

Jonathan knew that he was ready. It was as if a large net was spread out inside his head, ready to catch the words of the story as he heard them. All the rest of his life, he would be able to hold those words. One evening his father would begin to tell him the story. It would be an evening like this one, when they watched the sleeping desert together.

GOD SAID: "Let there be light…"

It is nearly dark.
Jonathan asks his father to tell
him about the first morning of the world.

The land was sleeping and the flock was quiet. Eliezer and his son Jonathan sat wrapped in their cloaks. The sky was still red over where the sun had set. Jonathan looked into the distance, and all he could see were vast stretches of stones and sand. There was not a sound. It was as if the world had not been born yet; as if not a single living creature had ever crossed those great empty spaces—as if tomorrow everything would begin.

Then Jonathan turned to his father: "Tell me what happened on the first morning of the world."

Eliezer closed his eyes. Not a muscle moved on his face. The words he was about to speak were spoken to him when he was Jonathan's age. They came slowly back to him from across all those years before they arrived there at his lips…

"No one saw the first morning of the world. It was a secret morning. For on that first morning of the world men and women had not yet been created. God alone saw that first morning. He saw it because it was He who caused it to be born. How He caused it to spring forth from His fingers no one can say exactly. It appeared suddenly and, in the hand of God, it was a thing brand new and innocent—a white bird, a cloud that skims the mountain. If a person had been there to see that first morning of the world, his whole face would have smiled at the sight of it, and in his eyes there would have blazed up a light so bright that nothing could ever again put it out.

"Look, Jonathan—the desert rests beneath the night. You will soon fall asleep too, and tomorrow, if you want to, you can rediscover that first morning. All you need to do is pretend you are waking up for the very first time. Gently, very gently, you open your eyes; you drink in the vastness of the sky, the vastness of the sands; then your eyes are drawn to a faint black thread running over the hills; it is the horizon. There are patches of light on your body. The feel of the air fluttering over your skin surprises you. A sound reaches your ears: it is from the water bubbling at the spring. But you do not know it is the spring, for its sound calls you for the first time. The world stands before you. You look at it, and you have the feeling that it is looking at you. It is as if an animal had come close to you while you were sleeping. As you wake up you catch sight of it calmly cropping the grass. It seems to be saying to you: 'Oh yes—take a good look at me! I am really here. Does that surprise you?'

"That is how the world was born on its first morning. It was a marvelous thing in the sight of God.

"However, don't start to think that there were already mountains, rivers, or flowers. At first there was nothing. Then, on that first morning, God created the sky and earth. The earth was formless and empty, mysterious and with no darkness, no light. As it left God's fingers it was a blind and deaf thing, but already full of hope and expectation. And God already knew that He loved it. There was no horizon, no shapes, neither heights nor depths. The sun did not exist, nor the seas. Yet God already knew what He was going to do to the earth. It was still gloomy, silent, and damp, but it was already precious in His eyes. I myself believe that God leaned over and hugged the earth.

"Then God set to work. He said the word, and each thing He named began to exist. 'Let there be light,' He said, and there was light. He pulled it away from the darkness and gave it a name: it was 'day.' And the darkness that had been separated from the light, that was 'night.' And only as God separated each thing from all others and gave it its own name—only then did it begin to be. He separated the land from the sea, the high

places from the low. He separated the vault of heaven from the abyss, and the waters of the rain from the waters of the sea…and everything began to be. Then God was happy. All that He had made was good. For the first time He could call out His name, hear it bounce off the earth, and then come back to Him like an echo."

God separated the
land from the sea,
the high places
from the low,
the vault of heaven
from the abyss.

GOD SAID: "Let there be lights in the firmament of heaven..."

Eliezer tells his son
about the first morning of the world,
when the earth was formless and empty,
without light and without night.

Jonathan had slept near the flock, and Eliezer had stayed awake part of the night to watch over the newborn lambs. There were still some good tufts of tall grass nearby, so they could stay where they were for a day or two. A tiny brook ran from a pile of rocks at the foot of a cliff, and Jonathan would go there soon to water the animals.

The moon disappeared and the stars faded. On the eastern horizon the line made by the hills became clearer. The great yellow disc would soon appear and would rise very quickly into the sky. The silent flock seemed to want the calm and rest of the night to last a little longer. Wrapped in their cloaks, Eliezer and Jonathan watched for the sun to come up. Jonathan asked, "Why doesn't the moon wait for the sun?"

Eliezer didn't answer, as if he had not heard the question. Suddenly the disc of the sun appeared, and rose right up into its path. Then Eliezer began speaking.

"The sun and the moon are like two sovereigns; God has given a kingdom to each. Both of them are proud to be rulers, but neither can take the other's place. God decided it should be this way when He made them.

"The sun is a stern empress, proud to show off her strength. She does not tolerate a single shadow to be near her. The moon is a great queen, always discreet. You will rarely see her by day, for she knows that she must not appear to challenge the empress.

"The sun speaks clearly; she must be obeyed. The moon knows about the subtle charm of diplomacy. She scribbles secrets onto old parchment, and whispers them into people's ears.

"The sun loves to be recognized and praised. The moon already knows that she is important, and needs no reminders; she is content to watch over the sleeping world with her round eye.

"The sun always proclaims what she has done: 'I bring light,' she says, 'and I chase away the night. I am reason and life.' Yet in the evening when she goes away satisfied with the work she has done, does she not realize that she leaves behind her a long, lifeless pause? It is then that the moon arrives and smiles. Like a night watchman, she silently takes her place, and keeps the night from being totally dark. Look carefully at the night: the shadows of the sand turn to blue and the rocks are lit with glints of white. The sun covers the hills

The sun and
the moon are like
two sovereigns.
God has given
a kingdom to each.

with gold, but at nightfall the moon quickly washes them clean with long streams of silver.

"The sun is vigorous and bountiful. The vines gorge themselves on her warmth, and crops drink in her light as they wait for their heavy harvests. Yet occasionally she becomes relentless and cruel. Like the lion, she rules the burning deserts. Then, during the cool night, the moon sweeps in to brush the violence away.

"That is how God made the sun and the moon to be. Each one is irreplaceable. As for yourself, take care not to treat them as though they were gods. It is God who created them and placed them at your service. The night, when you sleep and dream, is for you. Also for you is the day when you rise up and work. Thank God every day for the sun and the moon, for when they start their new journeys each day and night, it is done for you.

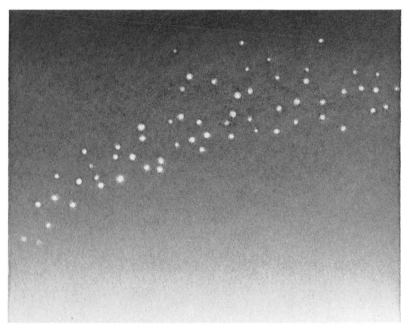

And above all, never forget the stars! Do you know that they signal to you from very far away? They are there for your joy. God has scattered them in handfuls across the dark night sky, where they glitter more brightly than diamonds."

GOD SAID: "Let the earth become green with growing things…"

*After hearing about the first morning
and the creation of the sun and the moon,
Jonathan asks his father how the plants were created.*

Eliezer and Jonathan had chosen a cleft in a large rock to shield themselves from the midday sun. The goats and sheep were stretched out on the sand, their flanks moving quickly in and out as they panted. The air shimmered in the heat, blurring the edges of everything in sight. Off in the distance they saw a mirage, a dancing image of trees and water. Jonathan asked his father how the plants were created.

"One day," began Eliezer, "I will take you away. We will leave here and travel north across the desert, and then up into the hills. We will walk for two days and rest on the third, and keep on like that to the end of the journey. We will pass the last hill, and there stretching away below us we shall find a vast plain covered with green. Trees grow there by the thousand, and bushes and flowers cover even the smallest scrap of ground. There are even plants which live at the bottom of rivers! You will be able to run to the trees, and you will hold in your hands fruits such as you have never seen.

"Then you will understand that when God first made the plants, it was a burst of joy. For on the day when

God said: 'Let the earth bring forth plants and trees,' the day when the earth began to grow green—that was life arriving on the earth and spreading everywhere: along the rivers, beside the seas and right up to the tops of the mountains. For plants are living things: they breathe,

they suffer from cold and heat, they can reproduce their own kind before they die.

"Your mother Sarah often says that trees and plants are the daughters of earth and sky. Do you know their seeds use the slightest breath of wind to set off on a journey through the air? Do you know that the palm tree

On the day the earth
began to grow green,
that was life
arriving on the earth
and spreading
everywhere.

is a curious creature that stretches up its neck to wave its head about in the wind? Plants may live in the air of the sky, but they are faithful to earth, for their roots secretly burrow in the soil to draw up their strength.

"When man and woman arrived on earth the trees and plants were waiting for them. There they were, providing shade and color, fruit and flowers. People realized they could not live without them, for they gave shelter, clothing, food, perfumes, and even healing balms. People also discovered that plants form a great protective cloak. See how the rain of a storm ravages the earth and scars it. Only the plants know how to calm the falling water, helping it sink drowsily into the ground and be transformed into gently bubbling springs.

"My father used to tell me that every plant has its own character. The cedar, he used to say, is proud and courageous. It lives close to the snows and dares to resist the storm, even at the cost of its life. The olive tree is a good friend. The vine is like a peasant, hardworking and solidly built. My father used to say something more: when someone shows you a new plant, gently pronounce its name as if you were greeting a friend, for that is how God greeted the growing things the day He made them. The names you learn will begin to sing in your head, and all your life you will take pleasure in repeating them: laurel and sycamore; balsam, myrtle and juniper; papyrus and sweet calamus; rock-rose, acacia; ginger and the cardamom seed; tamarisk, samphire, and sage.

"Once the name of a plant has sung in your head, you know that you must respect it. Never cut down a tree needlessly; it is as sad a thing to do as stopping up a spring. Never let a goat ravage a bush; it is as sad a thing as seeing a great fire devour a forest."

When man and
woman arrived
on earth the trees
and plants were
waiting for them.

GOD SAID: "Let birds fly above the earth…"

Eliezer enjoys teaching these things to Jonathan, and next he tells his son how God created the animals.

Eliezer and Jonathan returned to the main camp near a small oasis. They wanted to rest and spend a few days with family and friends before setting out again to graze the animals.

When they heard the flock, Jonathan's brothers and sisters and all his cousins ran to meet them, and soon they were wading and splashing in the water hole among the drinking sheep and goats.

Jonathan was happy. All day he had walked with his animals through the heat and dust, and now he was watching them drink. His ears were filled with bleatings and the pattering of hooves. A young goat frisked and splashed too close to a grumpy old ram, and was butted away with a great sweep of his head. Eliezer came out of the tent where he had gone to greet his wife Sarah. He saw Jonathan there watching the animals at the water hole, and came to stand next to him. He watched the animals for a few minutes before speaking.

"Can you imagine a world without animals? That would be a sad world! Even when you don't know it, animals are part of your life. Look way up there: do you see that still, dark speck in the sky, as small as a star? It is a hawk, and though he is always far away, he sees everything you do. There are gazelles over in the hills, their noses raised in the wind. You will never get close to them, yet they are there. Tonight while you sleep they will pass close by the tents. Your goats and sheep will know they are near, but all you will ever see are their footprints in the morning. Think of the gecko, the green lizard, or the cricket—all the little desert animals. They run from you by day, but during the night they come near, waking you sometimes with a faint rustle or quiet gnawing. Then you clap your hands to make the little animal run away, and you drift off to sleep again. Think of the stinging scorpion, or the horned viper who usually runs away, but is still dangerous. And as darkness falls, listen to the hyena's laughing cry or the strange wail of the jackal.

"At the beginning of the world God wanted the animals to live and multiply. The air, the sea, and the land needed to be humming with life before it was man's and woman's turn to arrive. So God said: 'Let the waters teem with a thousand different kinds of fish.' And the waters, like a mirror for His command, burst into life. Fish of every color—whole shoals at a time—started to chase each other through the waves. Some of them even flew with

God wanted
the animals to
live and multiply.

God put countless
animals on
the earth.

fins that worked like wings. And far, far below, the sea monsters lived in the depths.

"Next God said: 'Let birds populate the air all the way up to the sky.' And the air was filled with the rhythms of life. The clicking of beaks, pecking, cackling, cheeping, all blended into the familiar clamor of the skies. Some birds soared in the sunshine. Others ran along the ground for a long time before suddenly streaking up like arrows. Whole colonies of birds, gossiping and quarreling, covered the cliffs and islands. Meanwhile, great flocks of wading birds began to cross the sky, migrating to their summer feeding grounds. And right up to nightfall a chorus of feather-rustling, fluttering, and hooting rose to God's ears.

"Once the seas and the skies were full of the noise of all these living creatures, God put countless species of animals on the dry land as well. Then He was happy. He loved hearing all His creatures move and stir and mill about the world."

GOD SAID: "Be fruitful, multiply…"

*Eliezer tells Jonathan
that animals are not just servants,
but are true friends who knock
at the door of our dreams.*

Jonathan and his father Eliezer had been resting at the camp. At the end of the day, Eliezer talked with the other shepherds. They watched the sky uneasily, afraid that a sandstorm was coming. The sheep and the goats were much more nervous than usual.

Jonathan was watching over the flock. Eliezer shouted and told his son to collect all the animals before dark. Jonathan ran off to look for the stray goats, and when he found them, they seemed happy to be brought back. Meanwhile Eliezer had come out to be with the flock. He walked slowly among the animals, talking to them in his deep voice, calming them. Jonathan looked out over the desert. Nothing seemed to have changed: the sky was the same color and the sands were still. But the goats and sheep were stamping their hooves and milling about: clearly, they were uneasy.

"The wind is going to rise," said Eliezer. "The animals know it, and that is why they are so nervous. Animals always feel things before we do. You may not guess that rain or wind is about to hit you, but the animals have already felt it coming and are expecting it. They breathe the same air we do, and walk on the same ground, yet they have ways of knowing things that we don't have. They can see and feel things that are completely hidden from you and me.

"Animals have been on earth so long that they have a vast store of secret knowledge, and each generation hands it on to the next. An animal always spots danger before you do. When threatened, he knows immediately whether to fight, to flee, or in some other way defend himself. He instantly chooses the best response by instinct. That instinct is like a great inherited fortune, and each animal receives it and uses it, and when it is passed on, the fortune never gets smaller. Think of a lamb: the moment it comes out of its mother's womb it finds itself being licked by her and pushed with her muzzle to make it stand upright on its feet. Immediately that lamb begins to look for the mother's teats. It must do these things to survive. It has never learned these things, yet it knows them.

"Animals are more than just friends; they are our true companions here on the earth. And if we ever betrayed them, making them suffer or destroying them, we would be letting down our friends and fellow travelers. For they have journeyed just as far as we have—or even

farther—drinking at springs before man and woman drank there, sheltering in caves long before we came to them. They have received from God the same earth that we were given, with the same plants to eat, the same trees to live among, and the same sun to warm them.

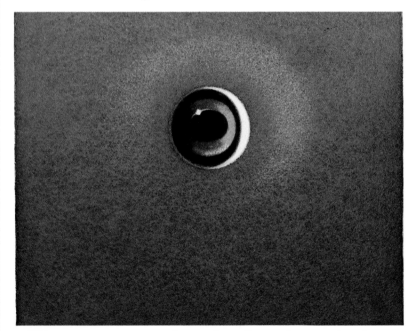

"If we ever came to the point of turning our backs on the animals, then we would be losing forever a part of ourselves, a hidden place within us where we could never again feel at home. That sudden anger that wells up uncontrollably inside you; that unexpected feeling of danger that upsets you; that intense longing to stay alive and to fight—all these feelings rise within you from a very, very long heritage. It is the animals that teach you to recognize and respect this heritage.

"Do you know why the animals knock so often at the door of our dreams? Very close, they silently pass before our eyes as we sleep, and disappear as the day breaks. I think I know why: They are just coming to visit us, like old friends who drop by to say hello. By day we think we are their masters, so by night they remind us that they have a secret life of their own that we can only dream of."

Do you know why the animals knock so often at the door of our dreams?

"GOD SAID: "Let us make man in our own image…"

*In the land of Canaan
two thousand five hundred years ago,
a father tells his son about the creation
of man and woman.*

The windstorm had blown all night. When he awoke, Jonathan ran to see the flock. The sheep and goats were all there, gathered round the water hole. Their fleeces were full of thick, yellow dust, but none had been harmed. Sarah, Jonathan's mother, had lit the fire. She kneaded dough and under her expert fingers it took the shape of a round griddle cake. As her son came towards her she raised her head and smiled at him. She had deep, black eyes.

Jonathan sat near the fire and watched his mother. When she did her work, she never seemed to have any problems, even when she had to do everything quickly. Jonathan spent most of his time tending the flock, far away from his mother. Yet he knew very well what a major part she played in the life of the family. He often thought of her when he was alone.

One day his father asked him: "What are you thinking about, Jonathan?"

"I am thinking about my mother," he replied. There was a long pause before his father broke the silence;

then he started in with this story.

"On the far side of the desert there are blue springs where neither the boldest adventurers nor the proudest conquerors have ever been able to lead their troops. Yet a man and woman go to drink there. The woman has

no belongings, the man is a barefooted beggar; yet when they join hands they can journey to the ends of the earth. What does it matter if the way is long, since they have patience? What does it matter if it is hard, since they have strength? In our language man is called "ish" and woman "isha." It is the same word, yet at the same time

God kneaded
some earth
over and over
again in His hands.
Then He formed
an earthen man.

it is different. For man and woman are both alike and different from one another, masculine and feminine, close and yet far apart.

"Now is the time for you to hear how God became the potter. The day when He wanted to create human beings He took some earth, kneaded it over and over again in His hands, and then made an earthen man. He gave him arms, legs, and a head, complete with nose, ears, mouth, and eyes. Then He blew into the nostrils of the earthen man to put breath into him, and the earthen man began to live. God saw his eyes open, his chest heave, his fingers move. God saw his head turn to the left and the right.

He was a living being on the earth.

"God had already made the animals in the same way. He modeled pieces of earth, blew into their nostrils, and the animals had become living creatures on the earth.

"But with the woman, God wanted her to be man's fellow creature. So He cast a very deep sleep upon man, and as he lay unconscious on the ground, God took a rib from his side.

"When man awoke, there at his side was woman, living and breathing. Man looked at her and said: 'Truly you are my fellow creature. We are made of the same flesh.' That is why man and woman seek one another and are drawn to one another. That is why it is so natural that they live together.

"One day, Jonathan, you will leave your mother and me. The wife you will have chosen, and who will have chosen you, will be at your side.

"And you will say to her: 'Look at me! I have no gold or silver to give you: I own nothing. Yet, what I do not have, I give you. That star shining deep within the water of the blue springs—let us go look for it; I give it to you. And also for you are the smooth brown stones along our way, the burning sands of the desert, the blue of the sky, the wind blowing in the night. And for you, all the hours and days that we will live together.'"

*When the man
awoke, the woman
at his side lived
and breathed.*

"GOD SAW everything that He had made, and, behold, it was very good."

*Eliezer tells how God invented rest
so that human beings might rule
the earth without despoiling it.*

Jonathan and Eliezer his father left the camp at daybreak. All day they had to drive the flock before them in search of new grazing grounds. Jonathan was feeling a little sad without exactly knowing why. The sheep and goats seemed quite sluggish and distracted. They had to be shouted at constantly to keep them moving ahead. The stragglers followed with their feet dragging and their heads nodding.

When the sun was directly overhead, it was time for a midday rest. Eliezer had noticed much earlier that Jonathan seemed quiet and downhearted today. Once they were settled in the shade of a large rock, Eliezer began to speak…

"The animals are sorry to leave the camp. They liked being near the water hole. And you, Jonathan—you are like them. I remember my father used to say that men and women were created on the same day as the animals, and that this is why they are so like them. Like the animals, men and women are affected by their own changing moods, by the flow of the seasons, by the elemental forces of water, air, earth, and fire.

Tomorrow your goats will run about like happy fools, and you too will rediscover how good it is to be alive…

"But really, men and women are not like the animals in everything. We have abilities beyond theirs, for as my father also used to tell me, animals were created in

the morning, and after that, towards evening, man and woman. And God said to them: 'I have put you on the earth last; you will be responsible for it. You are responsible for everything that exists.'

"There are animals stronger than we are, yet we are responsible for the earth. Many secrets of the universe

elude us, yet we still want to understand. We are constantly looking to the future. This rocky wasteland stretching out here before our eyes—who is to say that people will not make trees grow there one day? Who is to say that people will not one day live in the mountains, or that they will not go and touch the stars? God has told us to care for the earth. How can we be blamed if our desire is infinite? The earth is an immense gift offered to woman and to man. It has been given to us to explore, to love, to discover and transform.

"We can do anything we choose on the earth, with only this one exception: We may not despoil it. If we destroy life we are no longer God's stewards of the earth. For then the earth would once again become formless and empty, as it was at the beginning of the world, and people in their turn would disappear.

"That must be why God invented rest. Since man and woman were so dazzled by their own abilities, there was a risk that they would be obsessed with changing everything. Thinking they were in charge of all the earth, man and woman would certainly use it up and wear it out. God worked for six days to build the world. Yet there was another day, the seventh, a whole day during which He did nothing. And ever since that time, the seventh day is a breathing space for the universe. Make your

beast of burden carry all it truly can. But when the seventh day comes, lift off the pack-saddle that galls its back and let it wander at will. Asses also have the right to dream.

"That seventh day—it is like rain on dry ground, or like a long-awaited visit from a friend.

"One day man and woman will notice that they have grown old. So many times have they done and done again the same tasks, that their hands have become gnarled and their bodies bowed. So many times have they seen the sun rise and set on the desert sands that their eyes have become dim. Then they wash and perfume themselves, and put on their finest clothes before going to sit at the door of their tent. There they are, ready for the great and final seventh day. Above all, never believe that these old ones are sad. They know that it is a long, long journey for man and woman to develop the earth. Their children have become men and women in their turn, and it is they who now must journey on."

*You are responsible
for everything
that exists.*

MAN SAID: "I was afraid and I hid myself…"

But violence and fear worry Jonathan.
Where do they come from?
His father tells him stories that are full of meaning.

Once again Jonathan and Eliezer his father sat beneath the stars and looked out over the desert as it fell asleep. All around them there was life, abundant and invisible. They heard the cry of a clever fox, making plaintive little yelps as it left for the evening's hunting, as if weeping in advance for its own victims.

Eliezer had told the story of the beginning of the world over several days, and it was finished.

Jonathan understood it was over, but wished that it wasn't. "Tell me," he asked his father, "what will become of the world?"

Eliezer shook his head. "We do not know what will become of the world. My father did not know either. I remember asking him this question, and he only smiled, and began to tell me all sorts of short stories that were really like proverbs or fables. For example, he said, 'The human being is stone and sand. He was taken from the earth, but the blood flowing in his veins comes from the fire.' He also said, 'Some animals hunt during the day, others at night. Only human violence has no rest.'

"One day he even told me this strange story: 'An animal hid under a rock. Someone saw it and said: "It is a snake!" Then the snake killed him. Someone else came along and said: "It is a bird!" Then the bird flew away.' I often wonder about these stories. I do not understand why my father told them to me. But because they have

run through my mind so long, I have come to know them well, and bit by bit they have started to make sense. These are only little stories, and none of them is very important on its own. But taken together, they present a sort of picture of the world.

"Man and woman are unyielding and hard as if they

A conqueror sweeps across the plain, leading his armies. He captures a city.

were rock, but they are just as much like sand, shifting and moving about. When they die, the earth takes them back, because they were taken from the earth. However, something burns within them, like a longing that is never satisfied.

"The violence of the animals follows the rhythm of daytime and nighttime. The violence of people is very different, never stopping, unrelenting, capable of destroying everything.

"A conqueror sweeps across the plain, leading his armies. He captures a city, setting fire to the houses with all the people still inside them. His soldiers plunder and torture. To this conqueror the soldiers lead the defeated king with all his wives and children. They have had their eyes poked out.

"People live with violence: their future will depend upon how they learn to control it.

"I have often thought about the story of the snake and the bird. It is a very rich tale, and I am not sure if I have yet understood its full meaning. It means, I believe, that men and women have a great power: the ability to tame. If the violence that lies sleeping in the heart of a person makes you afraid, then that person will turn against you. However, if you see this same person and speak with him, calling him 'friend' and forgetting your fear, perhaps you will disarm his anger. Do not believe that the snake will always change itself into a bird. However, whenever you can, seek to tame it. All your days you will encounter violence. But remember! Every time you can, tame both beasts and people. Call everyone 'friend' so that they can learn to live in peace."

GENESIS,
THE FIRST BOOK OF THE BIBLE
an essay by Pierre-Marie Beaude,
Doctor of Theology,
Licentiate of the French Biblical Institute, Paris

The first book of the Bible is called Genesis. This is how it begins:

"In the beginning God created the heaven and the earth. Now the earth was without form, and void…" What follows is a very beautiful poem dedicated to the creation. God speaks and the world is born: day, night, the sky, the oceans, the plants, the animals, man and woman. And all is good.

Following upon this poem the Bible tells us the story of the creation a second time. This account is also very familiar to us, with the Garden of Eden, Adam, Eve coming from Adam's rib…After the creation the story continues with Adam and Eve being expelled from the garden, Cain and Abel, the Flood, the Tower of Babel. In all, eleven chapters of Genesis are devoted to the origins of humanity.

When were these accounts written?

They are derived from traditions handed down from mothers and fathers to sons and daughters. Then they were written down. The first poem is part of a longer whole which was put together in priestly circles about the time of the exile in Babylon (587-538 B.C.). The second account is the work of royal scribes, some of whom may already have been alive during the reign of King Solomon who died in 933 B.C. These details

are important. For instance, once we know that the first poem was written during the Exile, it seems to us a marvelous song of hope. In Babylon the exiles have lost everything: their country, their houses, their friends who had been killed during the capture of Jerusalem. How can they help despairing? Among them are some priests who refuse to accept that everything is finished. So they gather the ancient traditions of their people and form a story out of them. It is the God of Israel who has created the universe. It is He who made the sun and moon—which the Babylonians adore as gods—in order to give light to the world. This God is deserving of all trust. By respecting His laws we can look to the future with new hope.

What is the original element in Genesis?

Long before the Bible was born, all the great civilizations had their accounts of creation. A Babylonian poem entitled Enuma Elish and an epic poem called Atra-Hasis describe the creation of the world and human beings. The creation of humanity comes as the aftermath to a revolt of the lower gods whom seven higher gods had forced to do heavy labor. In this legend, it was human destiny to take on the burdens of the gods.

Though the ancient Near East seems to have been the cultural cradle of the Bible, the Bible itself is still distinctly original. In the poem Enuma Elish the world comes to birth as the outcome of a fight between Marduk and Tiamet. In the Bible there is no primordial fight, for the faith of Israel proclaims there is only one God. He creates the universe solely by the power of His word. He speaks and what He utters exists. Made in the image of God, men and women are not the slaves of the gods. Their mission is to be responsible for all the earth.

Are these accounts of any practical use?

In today's societies, these accounts play a fairly minor role when compared with the rational explanations of creation produced by science and technology. The Bible stories tend to be classified as wistful, fictional tales. In ancient societies, however, these narratives were intertwined with the preparations for every important moment in human existence—for starting the new year, for planting, for building, for setting off to war, etc. The biblical accounts served as basic explanations for human life: God takes woman from Adam's rib, and this means that woman is the equal of man; Cain, who killed his brother, builds the first city, and this means that violence lies at the heart of

our cities, at the heart of all humanity's independent enterprises. And the significance of God resting on the seventh day is that rest is essential to men and women, created as they are in God's image. Beneath the outward, literal presentations, the Bible accounts lay down the laws for a way of life.

Are the biblical accounts important to people in today's world?

These accounts from Genesis are thought to have little influence upon our thinking in this day and age. During that period when science and religion were in such confrontation, people were even able to think of them as worn-out legends.

In reality, the stories of the Bible have profoundly influenced our culture. We no longer believe that our world is a place where willful gods act out their battles. We no longer believe that individuals are subject to the blind forces of destiny. We no longer despair of ever seeing a day when all violence will cease.

Why? In large measure it is because the Bible texts have affirmed that all creation is the work of a good God, and that obedience to this good God frees men and women to find solutions for all their problems.

How did this book, "The Book of Creation" come to be written?

I imagined a father and son living in the desert about five centuries before Christ. For a long time I let the words of the Bible turn over in my mind and I arrived at another story, a new account, subordinate to, rather than a substitute for, the biblical one. Several times I recalled commentaries on these beautiful passages from the Jewish and Christian traditions. It was among some Jewish commentaries, for instance, that I found the idea of God listening to His name strike the earth, the idea that Adam's rib signifies his side, and the idea that the animals were created in the morning, while man and woman were created in the evening of the sixth day.

Finally, I would like to say how attached I have become to the characters in my story as they came to life beneath my pen. Along with them I, too, have come close to the secrets of existence. I am leaving this adventure more attentive to the rhythms of life, and with a deeper love of day and night, of water, earth, and sky. I have come to feel a real and deep unity with animals. Finally, I have been longing to say "Godspeed!" to man and woman, for in so many lands and over so many centuries, it is their story that forever begins anew.

oued asséché   végétation   petits ruisseaux

Questions Asked
of GEORGES LEMOINE
the Illustrator of this book
by CLAUDE RAISON

Georges Lemoine, how did the creation of the world come to be put into pictures?

A new book to illustrate! First and always, this is cause for happiness—an event, the promise of an adventure; it is good luck crossing one's path. It is also the near certainty that within this dwelling place for ideas that the writer has built, one will be able to find that private room, that hidden chamber in the center of it.

'The Book of Creation': a process of research during which old truths are discovered anew; months of work, a whole year of efforts, of disillusionments and, in the end, of hopes. Why hopes? Because from the pictures created, there comes to the mind a sweetness, a fragrance so real that it proves part of the race has been well and truly run.

A new picture—sometimes it is strange and empty, yet that very emptiness can also be beautiful. A picture—this is something that takes shape slowly; it is a fine sheet of 'd'Arches' paper, still untouched. It is extreme care. A picture—it is a word, a piece of music one hears, the piano of Debussey, the fingers of Marcelle Mayer, the calming voice of Ravi Shankar announcing a nocturne to be played on his sitar. It is all this. Dreams from the ends of the world... But also a drawing board. You put out the light, you shut the studio door till tomorrow, and then that restlessness in the morning when one must get on with the work.

You personally—do you like the desert?

The book was begun in February 1986, and in April of that year I went traveling in Israel so that I could cross the Negev. It had to be done. Without this trip, how could I have been truthful? With the help of books? Never! If you only knew...Those stones, those flowers in the clefts of rocks, that light, that sweetness! The sense that everything moves ahead, never backwards. It was there that I needed to discover my book, to learn about my characters, Jonathan and Eliezer...There we found one another. Yes, I love the desert!

Is there one picture in this book that you feel is more important than the others?

Perhaps the first, the one in which I wanted to show the creation being born out of darkness, out of nothingness, in its very first outlines. I love this picture; it has remained my point of reference right through this work. When I had to make choices, I made them with this picture in mind. This enabled me—at least that is my impression—to maintain a coherent vision straight through the course of the whole year's work. In my own way, I drew the first morning of the world, then I worked on until sunset.